Su
Clematis

WALTER HÖRSCH

Series Editor
LESLEY YOUNG

MEREHURST

Introduction

Clematis is becoming increasingly popular as a flowering garden climber. There are very few gardens indeed which do not have room or the ideal position in which one of the many varieties of clematis can be grown. Within just a few years of planting, walls, pergolas, espaliers and fences will be completely covered in a profusion of lovely flowers. Even old bushes and trees can act as a support for this charming plant. This guide will introduce you to several of the most beautiful clematis species and varieties, including both new and rare varieties as well as the well-loved, popular varieties. Clematis expert Walter Hörsch offers practical, knowledgeable advice on the choice of the right position, planting, care and pruning. He also explains what to do if your clematis is attacked by pests and diseases and how to propagate with the help of easily followed, step-by-step illustrations. Lovely colour photographs and interesting ideas for garden design demonstrate the versatility of this group of plants and will encourage the newcomer to clematis growing to experiment with ideas of their own.

Contents

Clematis montana "Rubens" with rhododendron.

"Rhapsody".

"Orange Peel".

The author
Walter Hörsch, by profession head teacher of a school for mechanics in Stuttgart, is an experienced gardener and a prominent member of the German section of the International Clematis Society.

The photographer
Marion Nickig is a well-known plant photographer who is famous for her unusual garden and flower photographs. Her work has been regularly published in both magazines and books for many years.

The illustrator
Marlene Gemke is a well-respected freelance artist who has contributed illustrations to many of the titles in the "Success with" gardening series.

NB: Please read the Author's notes on page 61 so that your enjoyment of clematis may remain unimpaired.

Botany and care

Beautiful colours, flowers as large as saucers or in small, nodding bells, luxuriantly growing tendrils and climbing shoots or bushy, compact container plants – clematis offer all this and more. Providing it has been planted properly and cared for well, a clematis variety or species will delight for weeks on end with its abundance of flowers.

Left: "Jackmanii" the oldest and probably best known clematis cultivar.
Above: "Jackmanii Alba", a semi-double variety with light green foliage.

5

Botany and care

The origin of the name "clematis"

Most representatives of this genus are woody climbing plants. Their botanical name *Clematis* is derived from the ancient Greek word "klema" which means "flexible shoot". The European name of forest vine refers to the preferred situation of the native European *Clematis vitalba* (also called old man's beard or traveller's joy) which grows mainly along the fringes of woodlands and in hedges. In early times the name "burn wort" was often used, as the juice of the clematis shoot contains an active substance called protoanemonin that may cause inflammation of the skin, irritates mucous membranes and results in a burning pain if it gets into an open wound. This plant was also called *"L'herbe aux gueux"* (beggars' herb) in France as beggars used to rub its juice on to their arms and legs to gain sympathy.

The distribution of clematis

Only three clematis species are native to central Europe:
- *Clematis vitalba* (traveller's joy)
- *Clematis alpina*
- *Clematis recta*, a shrubby plant with shoots that do not become woody.
Nowadays, gardeners are no longer restricted to growing only native species as there are about 200 clematis species worldwide, many of which feel quite at home in a European garden. Most of them originate from temperate regions of the world. Many of the best-known examples come from

The naming of clematis species and varieties

Clematis species are the original wild vines, also referred to as wild forms. They are the original plants from which all others have been cultivated. The genus name and species name are written in italic print, for example: *Clematis viticella*. Clematis varieties and hybrids are cultivars that were created through selection or the crossing of specimens with beautiful flowers, new colours or longer-lasting flowers. Most of the large-flowered garden varieties are included among the clematis cultivars mentioned in this volume. The variety name is generally written within quotation marks; for example, *Clematis alpina* "Frances Rivis" and *Clematis* "Jackmanii".

China (*Clematis montana*), Japan (*Clematis patens*) and North America (*Clematis texensis*).

The history of clematis cultivation

As early as the seventeenth century, a few foreign species, like the dainty Italian vine (*Clematis viticella*), were known in central Europe. The famous *Florilegium* of Basilius Besler, published in 1613, depicts clematis in shades of red and blue, with both single and double flowers. In the nineteenth century, the available selection of clematis expanded greatly as plant collectors brought back species and seeds from China, Japan and North America. In 1839, the *Blumen-Zeitung*, published in Thuringia, reported that the beautiful *Clematis florida* "Sieboldii" was in bloom in the Kunst and Handelsgärtnerei Haage (a plant nursery) in Erfurt.

A romantic clematis-covered retreat.

The arrival of large-flowered garden varieties

The large-flowered *Clematis* "Jackmanii" was developed in the Jackman tree nursery in Woking, England. It created a sensation at the time and is still one of the most popular clematis forms. Its great success unleashed a veritable clematis craze and British cultivators, in particular, created many new garden varieties that are still available today. At the beginning of the twentieth century, however, clematis fever died down somewhat, partly because of the outbreak of the First World War, but also because of the spread of the disease called clematis wilt (see p. 22). Over the last twenty years, interest in this versatile climbing plant has experienced a revival. Raisers like Fisk and Pennell in Britain, Noll and Franczak in Poland and Keay in New Zealand have given us many new clematis varieties. The partners for crossing to produce all these hybrids are *Clematis viticella*, *Clematis lanuginosa*, *Clematis florida* and *Clematis patens*.

Botany

Shapes of growth

Most clematis forms are woody climbing plants. There are also herbaceous perennial types, such as the upright *Clematis recta*, whose shoots above ground die off in the autumn and which produces new shoots the following year. Some of the climbing forms, like *Clematis armandii*, are evergreen but most lose their foliage in the autumn. While some vigorously growing species, like *Clematis montana* and the native European *Clematis vitalba*, attain heights of up to 10 m (33 ft), many garden varieties are of medium or low height. Most clematis are extremely longlived and may live for decades.

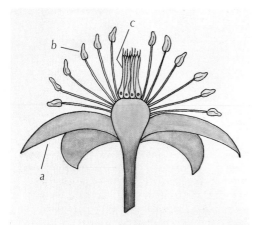

1 The structure of the flower: a) petals;
b) stamen with anther and filament; c) pistil with
stigma, style and ovary.

Flowers
(illustrations 1 and 2)

The structure of the flower
(illustration 1)
Clematis have simple petal structures which are not divided up into petals and sepals. At the centre of the flower, masses of male stamens surround equally numerous female organs. The insects that are responsible for pollination are mostly attracted by the colour of the flowers, only a few of which, for example *Clematis montana* "Wilsonii", release a definite scent. After the flowers have faded, many clematis, the wild species in particular, develop a bushy, feathery seedhead.

Flower shapes
(illustrations 2a-2e)
The flowers of this genus display great variation in their shapes and sizes. The wild species often have very delicate flowers while the numerous garden varieties form large, open, flat, saucer-like flowers which can be as wide as 20 cm (8 in)

2 Shapes of flowers:
a) saucer-shaped
flower.

across. Among the garden varieties, specimens with double flowers can be found and there are also bell-shaped and pitcher-shaped flowers. The flowers often have long stalks and grow from leaf axils and on the ends of shoots.

Colours of flowers:
The range of colours found in clematis flowers extends from the most delicate pink and palest blue via velvety shades of deep blue and red right through to shining white. Some small-flowered species also come in shades of yellow. In some cultivars, the petals may also have a central stripe in a different colour.

b) saucer-shaped, double flower.

c) star-shaped flower.

d) nodding flower with pointed petals.

e) bell-shaped flower.

Flowering time:

Generally speaking, clematis can be divided into:
● spring-flowering types.
● early-summer-flowering types
● summer-flowering types.
There are also some extremely early-flowering species like *Clematis napaulensis* which flowers around the turn of the year. On the other hand, certain other species, like *Clematis lasiandra*, do not flower until the second month of autumn. The early-summer-flowering types and some species, for example *Clematis alpina*, will flower a second time, provided weather conditions are favourable, during the last month of summer/early autumn. You must remember, however, that the flowering time, length of flowering time and the colouring of a species or garden variety may vary depending on the soil conditions, climate and position in which it is growing.

Leaves

Depending on the species, the leaves too may have very different shapes and may be tripartite, feathery or simple. They grow in alternating pairs and their stalks are sensitive to touch. In the climbing forms, the stalks and tendrils are also climbing organs which wrap themselves round supports and help the clematis to reach great heights and resist the tugging of the wind.

Climbing techniques
(illustration 3)

The climbers among clematis belong to the group of plants that climb with the help of adapted leaf stalks. In their natural environments, in hedges or along the edges of woodland, they are able to use these climbing organs to reach the light. They wrap their leaf stalks around thin twigs and branches of bushes or trees and make use of any hold. In the autumn, only the leaves drop off; the shoots become woody and last through the winter.

3 Climbing organs:
The leaf stalks wind around the support.

Botany and care

"Madame Julia Correvon" has particularly profuse and longlasting flowers.

Buying clematis

Even if you are greatly tempted by the sight of beautiful flowers, you must give some thought to exactly what you want to achieve and to the conditions in which the plant of your choice must live. This will save you any later disappointment.
Ask yourself the following questions before buying.

When will the plant flower?
The flowering time of clematis will vary according to the species or variety. Clematis can be roughly divided into three groups:
A: spring-flowering (second and third months of spring)
B: early-summer-flowering (first month of summer)
C: summer-flowering (second month of summer and later).

How tall do you wish your clematis to grow?
The height of growth will play an important role in your choice of species.
● The herbaceous perennial clematis types grow only to about 1 m (40 in) tall.
● Most climbing clematis attain a height of 3 m (10 ft) or more. There are also slow-growing types which are suitable for

growing in a large container.

● Particularly fast-growing clematis, which can grow up to 10 m (33 ft) tall, include *Clematis vitalba* and *Clematis montana* and their varieties.

Large or small flowers?

The size and colour of the flowers are also important considerations when choosing a plant. Large flowers in wonderful colours are found among the early-summer-flowering and summer-flowering clematis (see pp. 38-57). All other clematis have more delicate flowers and are particularly suited to a nature garden.

Make sure that the plant you buy has a label giving its correct botanical name. Unfortunately, there are still some places which offer these plants for sale bearing labels such as "Clematis red". As a beginner, you should leave these plants alone. Only if you know the species or variety name will you be able to find information on the correct way to prune (see pp. 16/17).

Nowadays, clematis are usually offered for sale in plastic pots or containers.

● Clematis in small pots are better priced but will take longer to produce plenty of flowers. Often, it is better to let weaker plants spend several months growing in a larger pot before planting them in their final position.

● Clematis in larger containers have generally spent their early

life in a nursery and can be planted out right away. An additional advantage with larger plants is that they are often already in bloom at the nursery or garden centre, which will make choosing a lot easier.

Plant nurseries and garden centres

You will usually find a standard selection of popular, tried and tested clematis varieties in plant nurseries, tree nurseries and garden centres. If you have a special or rare plant in mind, however, you may find that you are unable to obtain it in your local garden centre or nursery. In that case, it is worth trying a mail-order tree nursery which should have a large selection of clematis varieties and may be able to meet your demands. In very special cases, you might even need to turn to tree nurseries abroad but this could prove expensive.

The right position

Light, heat, soil consistency and moisture will all influence the well-being of clematis.

Light: As clematis grow naturally in the semi-shade of forest edges, they also like a bright to semi-shady position in a garden. Extremely hot, south-facing positions will create problems.

Soil: In principle, the large-flowering garden varieties make greater demands on the quality of the soil than the wild species. All prefer a permeable, nutrient-rich soil (see pp. 12/13).

Moisture: Choose a position that is easy to water during the summer as clematis require plenty of water. Good drainage is also particularly important as clematis are very sensitive to waterlogging. It may be necessary to install proper drainage if you plant in heavy soil (see pp. 12/13).

Further information on the special requirements of the various different species and varieties is supplied in the plant descriptions on pages 36-57.

My tip: If you describe your garden or, better still, take along some photographs or a diagram, a good nurseryman should be able to offer advice on suitable species for you to choose from. Mail order catalogues often have a telephone number for enquiries. If you call them, they can also usually offer sound advice on which variety to choose.

Planting clematis

The best planting times for clematis are autumn and spring. As these plants are now offered for sale in pots almost all year round, you can also plant them at other times too, providing the soil is not frozen or dried out to a great depth after a long period of drought.

Planting outside
(illustrations 1a and 1b)

Digging the planting hole
Clematis form an extensive root system and require plenty of water and nutrients. The planting hole should, therefore, be made large enough and should normally be about 40 cm (16 in) wide and 40 cm (16 in) deep. It should only be smaller than this if the soil is of excellent quality.

Preparing the soil and the plant
● Loosen the soil at the bottom of the hole and on the walls. If the soil is very heavy, improve the drainage in the floor of the hole by inserting a layer of gravel to prevent waterlogging.
● Shovel in some good quality garden soil mixed with garden compost or cattle dung (both well rotted) and well-moistened peat. Add two handfuls of organic compound fertilizer as a controlled-release fertilizer.
● Water the rootstock thoroughly by allowing the pot to stand in a container of water for ten to twenty minutes.

Planting
● Carefully remove the clematis and its rootstock from the pot. In the case of most clematis species, leave the rootstock as undisturbed as possible, as the roots are particularly fine and sensitive. In some varieties the outer roots may be distributed a little around the planting hole.
● Place the clematis, together with its support stick, in the centre of the planting hole so that the top edge of the rootstock ends up about 5 cm (2 in) beneath the surface of the soil.
● Plants that are to be trained up a wall should be placed slightly at an angle towards the wall. Make sure that the plant is about 40 cm (16 in) away from the wall so that the roots will be reached by rainwater (see illustration 1a).
● If the clematis is meant to climb up a bush or tree, plant it at the outer edge of the root system of the supporting tree (see illustration 1b). In the case of large, mature trees, you may also dig a planting hole right beside the trunk.
● Shovel the prepared soil all around the rootstock and press the soil down carefully but firmly.
● Water the plant well.
● Now drive a climbing stick into the soil beside the rootstock and connect it to the support stick which should have been supplied with the clematis in the pot. Make the attachment at

1 Planting outside:
a) Plant the clematis leaning towards the wall.
b) Train the plant towards the branches of a tree.

2 Provide shade for the area around the root:
a) *Cover the soil with stones.*
b) *Underplant with low-growing plants.*

the point towards which you want the clematis to grow.

Give a little extra care and attention to this new plant in your garden until you are sure it has established itself.

Water regularly and tie up the very fragile shoots with raffia or sisal string.

NB: While carrying out these jobs, take care not to bend or break the sensitive shoots as fungus spores may easily penetrate the damaged places and infect the plant (see pp. 22/23).

Creating shade around the planting surface
(illustrations 2a and 2b)

Clematis require cool, shady "feet". This can be ensured in several different ways.
● The planting surface can be covered up with well-rotted compost, bark mulch (make sure it is at least 10 cm or 4 in away from any shoots) or cover the area with large stones (see illustration 2a).
● Underplanting with low-growing plants like lavender (*Lavandula*), heather (*Calluna*), species of *Potentilla* that remain small or shrubby *Hebe* will also provide shade (see illustration 2b).

Planting in a large container
(illustration 3)

When choosing a container, consider the height to which the clematis will grow. The plant container should have a diameter of at least 30 cm (12 in) and a height of at least 40 cm (16 in). If possible, choose a clay or wooden container with several, not too small, drainage holes. In plastic pots, the roots of clematis are subject to too much heat in the summer and too much cold in the winter.

Method
● Cover the drainage hole with a potshard and place a 6 cm (2¼ in) thick layer of Hortag or gravel in the bottom of the pot.
● Enrich good garden soil with garden compost or cow dung (both well rotted) and well-moistened peat. Add two handfuls of an organic compound fertilizer.
● Place 5-10 cm (2-4 in) of the compost in the pot.
● Place the plant and climbing aid in the container and train the

clematis up the support stick.
● Add the rest of the compost and water carefully.
● Water daily and, after the plant has acclimatized to the container, fertilize once a week with liquid fertilizer.

3 *In a large container, a drainage layer will prevent waterlogging.*

Botany and care

Care all year round

Clematis needs to be provided with plenty of water and nutrients in order to thrive and produce lots of flowers. In addition, many varieties require an annual pruning and the occasional tying up of new shoots.

Watering

Clematis have to supply their widely spreading foliage with water and nutrients. During the growth period (from mid-spring to late summer) additional watering will therefore become most important. Give a full watering can (10 litres/2¼ gal) of water every eight days during dry periods.
The following plants will require more frequent watering:
● young plants
● plants in sunny positions
● plants in very permeable soil.
Make sure that you do not wet the foliage and flowers when watering.

Fertilizing

Organic fertilizer, such as garden compost or cow dung (both well rotted), hoof/horn or organic compound fertilizer will supply nutrients and trace elements. These fertilizers work slowly but do improve the quality of the soil.

Mineral compound fertilizers contain the main nutrients of nitrogen (N), phosphorus (P) and potassium (K) as well as all necessary trace elements.
● Solid fertilizer should be carefully mixed with the soil (water well beforehand) and will gradually release nutrients to the plant.
● Liquid fertilizers work very fast but they may be washed away in heavy rains to end up in the ground water.
● Mineral compound fertilizers work fast and intensely. Too much of them may do more harm than good.

Fertilizing in the spring
During the formation of new shoots in the spring, the nutrient requirements of clematis will be particularly high. This is why a starter dose of fertilizer will be needed around the first month of spring.
● Very carefully, loosen the soil a little all around the plant and work in about two handfuls of nitrogen-based compound fertilizer or a handful of mineral compound fertilizer.
● Then mulch with garden compost or cow dung (both well rotted) all around the plant. Make sure there is a space of at least 10 cm (4 in) between the mulch and the shoots.

Fertilizing during the growth phase
During the main growth phase, you can give the plant liquid fertilizer weekly according to the manufacturer's instructions. Do not fertilize when the clematis is in flower as this would shorten the flowering time.

Climbing aids

Wherever the young shoots are unable to gain a hold, they will require regular loose tying up with raffia, sisal string or plastic-coated wire. If you do not do this, you may find that the clematis slides downwards into a single, muddled ball of foliage and flowers.

Winter protection

In cooler regions, we recommend that you provide winter protection for young clematis plants, in particular, by covering them with straw or brushwood. Clematis in large containers are best overwintered in a frost-free, bright room.

Clematis tibetana vernayi "Orange Peel" produces masses of flowers and grows vigorously. Its nodding, yellow flowers form particularly bushy seedheads.

Pruning clematis

A planting cut and annual pruning are important measures to maintain strong, healthy plants.

The planting cut
(illustration 1)

Most clematis have to be cut back during their first year. This will encourage the plant to branch out and it will grow stronger and become less susceptible to damage through breaking. If you are planting in the autumn, cut the shoots back to 25 cm (10 in) towards the end of autumn. If you have

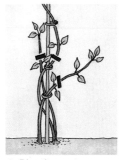

1 Planting cut:
Prune after planting.

planted in the spring, pruning can be carried out immediately after planting.

The annual pruning

Many clematis are cut back annually in order to curb excessive growth and to encourage branching out and the formation of flowers. Clematis can be divided into three groups, depending on their manner of flowering, and these require different pruning measures.

Pruning spring-flowering clematis
(Group A)
(illustration 2a)

Plants from this group flower from the second to third months of spring.
This group includes *Clematis alpina*, *Clematis macropetala* and *Clematis montana* and their varieties.

Plants from this group do not require cutting back.
● Immediately after flowering, merely remove dead or weak shoots.
● Plants that have become too large can also be thinned out immediately after flowering. They will then form new shoots that flower the following year.

Cutting early-summer-flowering clematis
(Group B)
(illustration 2b)

Plants from this group flower from the end of the last month of spring into the first month of summer on shoots from the previous year. This group includes *Clematis florida*, *Clematis patens* as well as *Clematis languinosa*. Under favourable conditions, they will flower again in the last month of summer and early autumn. This clematis should be cut back in late autumn.
● Remove dead and weak shoots.

2 Annual pruning groups:
A Spring-flowering clematis: remove all dead parts.

● Cut back the other shoots at the tips by 10-20 cm (4-8 in) to the next leaf axil. The new flowers will grow out of these axils during the following late spring.
● While pruning, tie back the shoots in such a way that they are not too close together. Ensure that the loops are not too tightly bound round the plant stems.

B Early-summer-flowering clematis requires less pruning in autumn.

C Summer-flowering clematis requires radical pruning in autumn.

Pruning summer-flowering clematis

(Group C)
(illustration 2c)

Plants from this group flower during the second month of summer and, later, from the fresh shoots of the current year. This group includes derivatives of the *Jackmanii viticelli* and *texensis* groups and also herbaceous perennial clematis. Clematis from this group should be cut back vigorously in late autumn.

● Plants that grow on a house wall, fence or pergola can be cut back to about 20 cm (8 in) above the ground. This will ensure that the flowers that appear on shoot tips in the summer are about eye level.
● Herbaceous perennial clematis must also be cut back radically. Its vigorous growth will ensure that it attains its original height and spread at flowering time.

My tip: If clematis of this group grow into a tree or bush you should be careful when pruning. Shorten only some of the shoots to 50-100 cm (20-40 in) above the ground and allow the others to continue growing. This will ensure that you end up with flowers evenly distributed over the entire height.

The main rules of pruning

(illustration 3)

The same rules of pruning that apply to other woody plants also apply to the pruning of clematis.
● Cut a few millimetres above a pair of buds – not too low (see illustration 3a) and not too high (see illustration 3b).
● The cuttting surface should be on a slant to prevent water from lying on it, which could bring about a risk of infection for the plant.
● Use only sharp tools so that the cut is smooth.
● Make sure your tools are clean. Always disinfect cutting tools with alcohol after working with other plants.

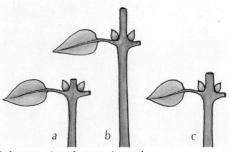

3 Incorrect and correct pruning:
a) *Space between cut and buds too small;*
b) *too large; c) correct – just above a pair of buds.*

A vision in purple and delicate pink – Clematis "Rhapsody" combined with the densely double bush rose "Heritage".

Propagating clematis

The simplest and quickest way to enlarge your stock of clematis plants is probably to visit the nearest nursery and buy to your heart's content. However, there are other options to consider. What keen clematis grower would not be tempted to grow his or her own plants in order to enlarge their stock of clematis? Perhaps you have discovered an attractive speciman that you particularly like in the garden of a friend. This is the moment to try to grow another plant from it. Clematis can be propagated vegetatively (non-sexually) or generatively (sexually).

Vegetative propagation

In the case of non-sexual propagation, new specimens can be obtained from parts of a single plant, the parent plant. This method has an advantage over the sexual (generative) method of growing from seed in that the descendants resemble the parent plant in all respects because their genetic material is identical. The following vegetative propagation methods are possible with clematis.

By layering downward-hanging shoots: This method is suitable for climbing clematis types and is the simplest method for beginners.

Propagation from cuttings: This is particularly promising for the amateur gardener with *Clematis alpina, Clematis macropetala* and *Clematis montana* and their varieties. In addition to grafting, some tree nurseries also propagate from the large-flowered garden varieties by taking cuttings.

By division: This method, in which the rootstock of the plant is divided, is only suitable for herbaceous perennial clematis. The three possible methods of vegetative propagation are explained in detail on pages 20 and 21.

By grafting: Many garden varieties that can be bought in a tree nursery or in a garden centre have been created through grafting.
Bud-bearing parts of the desired clematis are joined with a stock (generally *Clematis vitalba*) and allowed to fuse together. This procedure does, however, require special knowledge and is not suitable for the amateur to attempt.

Generative propagation

If pollen from one plant arrives on the stigma of a flower of another plant of the same species, seed will form. This sexual (or generative) propagation creates new plants that have genetic material that is not identical to that of the parent plants. The transfer of pollen to the stigma in clematis is not primarily carried out by insects as it is in other genera of plants but, instead, is achieved through the raiser's intervention.

In nature, but also often in undisturbed corners of the garden, new plants are created from the falling seed. This is, without doubt, the most convenient way to propagate. However, the targeted sowing of ripe seed may also often lead to success, although the germination time may vary considerably depending on the species or variety involved. Instructions on how to sow seed are given on page 21. Note that plants derived from seed are not identical to the parent plants. Raisers often obtain completely new varieties by transferring the pollen from one clematis variety or species to the stigma of another.

Propagating clematis

With a little patience and knowledge, many clematis varieties can be propagated successfully by the amateur gardener.

Layering downward-hanging shoots

(illustrations 1a and 1b)

Here, a shoot is encouraged to form roots.

Method
● Choose a shoot that is no longer soft and green but fully grown, for example from the previous year.
● Fill a flowerpot (with a diameter of about 12 cm or 4¾ in) with a mixture of good garden soil and peat and sink the pot into the soil up to its rim.
● Now place the shoot at a slant in the pot and carefully fix it with a wire pin.

2 Cuttings:
a) Plant the cutting in a pot.

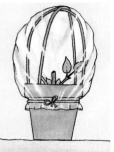

b) To encourage root formation, draw a transparent plastic bag over a wire frame.

● Insert a stick in the pot and carefully tie the tip of the shoot to it. The shoot should have produced its own roots after eight or nine months.
● Separate the new plant from the old shoot and shorten the tip of the shoot to about 15 cm (6 in).
● Remove the pot from the soil and plant the young plant in a larger pot filled with good garden soil.
● About six months later, the new clematis will be ready to be planted out.

My tip: Root formation is encouraged if you make a careful, diagonal incision from

below at the lowest point in the shoot being layered and dust this cut with rooting powder.

Division

Herbaceous perennial clematis, like *Clematis integrifolia*, can be propagated from a simple division of the rootstock. To do this, dig out the root in the autumn, carefully divide it into two or three sections and replant them.

1 Layering:
a) Peg a downward-hanging shoot into a pot.

b) Separate the rooted shoot from the parent plant.

Taking cuttings

(illustrations 2a and 2b)

Clematis are frequently propagated from cuttings. As a beginner, you are most likely to be successful with *Clematis alpina*, *Clematis macropetala* or *Clematis montana* as these species root more easily than the large-flowering varieties.

Method

● During the last month of spring/first month of summer, cut off a mature but not too woody clematis shoot.

● Divide this by making one diagonal cut just above a pair of leaves and another about 4-5 cm (1½-2 in) below it.

● Reduce the amount of foliage by cutting off one leaf completely and removing those parts of the second one that would later lie on the surface of the soil, and then stand the cutting in water for a short time.

● Fill a clay pot with planting compost made up of equal parts of peat and sand and press down lightly. An additional 2 cm (¾ in) thick layer of clean sand on top will prevent moss from growing on the surface.

● Now insert the cutting into the compost right up to where the leaves emerge, water and place a transparent plastic bag over the pot. The use of rooting powder will speed up the process of development.

● Stand the pot in a bright (not sunny) and warm position. 22° C (72° F) is ideal. After four to eight weeks, the cuttings should have rooted properly.

● Now plant the young plants in a pot that is not too large and filled with good quality, only lightly fertilized garden soil mixed with peat.

Sowing seed

(illustrations 3a-3c)

For sowing seed you will require pots or seed trays as well as seeding compost.

● Harvest ripe seedheads as soon as they are easy to remove and discard the hairs.

● Fill the pots or seed trays with seeding compost and distribute the seeds evenly and not too close together.

● Then, cover the seeds with a thin layer of compost and water lightly with a spray attachment.

The best plan is to keep the pots in a cold frame or propagator in a bright but not too sunny position until they germinate (this may take up to a year). Make sure the compost never dries out.

After the seed has germinated, stand the pots or propagator in a brighter position and air frequently.

● Once the young plants are about 3 cm (1¼ in) tall, prick them out singly into small pots. When they start to climb, they should be supplied with support sticks and should be planted out after one year.

My tip: Pinch out the shoot tips several times to obtain strong, bushy growth in the young plants.

3 a) *Sow the seed, cover it and stand in a bright position.*

b) *When the seedlings are about 3 cm (1¼ in) tall, prick them out.*

c) *Once they begin to climb, plant them in a larger container.*

Botany and care

Pests and diseases

Careful planting and care will create disease-resistant plants. Damage caused by pests and diseases that may still occur can be avoided through vigilance.

Pests

Compared with other plants, noticeably few pests bother clematis.

Slugs and snails: If you do not watch carefully, slugs and snails may devour entire plants, particularly young ones. The danger is greatest just after rain. Snails are rarely active during hot, sunny weather.

Remedy

● Collect the slugs and snails in the mornings and evenings.

● Install beer traps by burying plastic cartons up to their rims in the soil and filling them with beer. The slugs and snails will be tempted by the smell and will drown in the beer. Make sure very young children or dogs cannot get to the beer.

● Only if the problem is really severe should you resort to slug pellets. Do not use these at all if you have domestic pets. Collect the dead slugs to prevent birds from eating them and being poisoned.

Earwigs: These are active at night and like to eat the delicate leaves, flowers and buds of clematis.

Remedy: With the help of a torch, collect the earwigs at night or in the morning from under planks of wood, pieces of bark and upside-down flowerpots that have been left out on purpose near damaged plants to provide shelter for them.

Aphids: These may appear occasionally, particularly on the undersides of leaves and on young shoots.

Remedy: Wash the aphids off with water or spray them with a biological soap solution. If the infestation is severe, spray with an agent containing pyrethrum but handle this with care and be aware that it will kill useful insects, bees and fish.

Diseases

Very few serious diseases occur among clematis. In addition to powdery mildew and grey mould, the most dreaded disease is clematis wilt.

Clematis wilt

Leaves and flowers that suddenly hang limply are the first symptoms of clematis wilt. Within a few days, the shoots will wilt and turn brown. The cause is a fungus which attacks the plant just above the surface of the soil. The conduction of water and sap is interrupted and the shoots die. The large-flowered cultivars are most at risk, while wild species and strong, healthy plants are less susceptible.

Remedy: Once clematis wilt has appeared it cannot be prevented.

● Cut off the shoots right down to ground level and destroy them. Do not discard them on your compost heap! In most cases, the clematis will produce shoots again, although sometimes not until the following year.

● If infestation occurs frequently, fungicidal chemical sprays can be employed at monthly intervals according to the manufacturer's instructions.

My tip: Do not buy plants with bent or broken shoots and avoid damaging the clematis when tying it. Fungal spores find damaged shoots an ideal means of access.

Other fungal diseases

Plants growing too densely together, high humidity, excess nitrogen fertilization and muggy weather all encourage fungal diseases.

Powdery mildew: This coats parts of the plant with a whitish film.

Grey mould: This forms a brownish-grey film on leaves, stalks and flowers.

Remedy: Remove affected parts and destroy them (do not compost them). Spray according

The shrubby, upright-growing Clematis recta is indigenous to Europe.

to the manufacturer's instructions with agents that combat these diseases.

Handling plant protection agents

● Do not employ highly toxic agents.

● Follow manufacterers' instructions and recommended doses meticulously.

● When spraying, wear rubber gloves, do not eat, drink or smoke. Do not inhale spray.

● Only spray on calm days so that the agent is not blown on to a neighbour's property.

● Always keep plant protection agents in their original packaging and never together with foodstuffs or in a place that is easily accessible to children or domestic pets.

Enchanting ideas for planting

The opportunities for employing clematis as an ornament around the house and garden are extensive. You can use it to create romantic garden settings and can emphasize its beautiful, exotic flowers by growing attractive accompanying plants.

Left: a popular beauty - "Comtesse de Bouchaud" has mallow pink, saucer-shaped flowers.
Above: "Walter Pennell" is a semi-double variety with light-coloured stamens.

Garden design

Natural climbers

Clematis are particularly sociable plants. In their natural environment they will climb over trees and bushes – a habit which you should bear in mind when choosing the right position for your clematis.

Clematis in trees

Particularly vigorously growing clematis are suitable for climbing through evergreen trees like yew (*Taxus baccata*), pines (*Pinus*), spruce (*Picea*), Lawson cypress (*Chamaecyparis lawsoniana*), arbor-vitae (*Thuja occidentalis*) or eastern hemlock (*Tsuga canadensis*). These include *Clematis montana* and its varieties, *Clematis chrysocoma* var. *sericea*, *Clematis potaninii* var. *potaninii*, *Clematis flammula*, *Clematis tibetana vernayi* (syn. *Clematis orientalis*) and *Clematis tangutica*.
Instructions on the correct planting procedure and training on to the support can be found on pages 12/13. *Clematis viticella* and its varieties are particularly suitable for low-growing, deciduous trees like ornamental cherry (*Prunus cerasifera*), apple (*Mallus*), pear (*Pyrus salicifolia*) or oleaster (*Eleagnus angustifolia*). The large-flowered clematis varieties like "Ascotiensis", "Ernest Markham", "Gipsy Queen",

"Huldine" and "Perle d'Azur" are also used for climbing through smaller trees. Two particularly attractive combinations are given below.
● The dark violet flowers of *Clematis viticella* "Etoile Violette" or the deep purple red flowers of *Clematis viticella* "Royal Velours" look extremely effective in a locust tree with its yellow leaves (*Robinia pseudoacacia* "Frisia").
● Light blue *Clematis* "Perle d'Azur" or the lovely pink *Clematis* "Hagley Hybrid" look wonderful growing in a red-leafed ornamental cherry (*Prunus cerasifera*).

Clematis growing in bushes

Many bushes are ideal partners for the large-flowered clematis varieties and also for slow-growing species like *Clematis alpina* or *Clematis macropetala*. As these species hardly need any pruning, they should only be combined with bushes that also require no cutting back.
Suitable natural climbing aids for clematis include rhododendron (*Rhododendron*), cherry laurel (*Prunus laurocerasus*), *Spiraea*, snowberry (*Symphoricarpos*), lilac (*Syringa microphylla* "Superba"), *Caryopteris incana*, *Perovskia abrotanoides* or winter heather (*Erica carnea* hybrids). The dark-coloured flowers of certain clematis varieties form an

attractive contrast to bushes with light-coloured foliage. For example, *Clematis viticella* "Etoile Violette" or "Polish Spirit" look particularly good in a maple (*Acer negundo* "Flamingo") with its white-flecked leaves which have a hint of pink.
Further beautiful combinations include:
● *Clematis* "Huldine" with a viburnum (*Viburnum* x *pragense*)
● *Clematis texensis* "Sir Trevor Lawrence" with cotoneaster (*Cotoneaster horizontalis*)
● *Clematis versicolor* in a magnolia (*Magnolia stellata*)
● double-flowering clematis varieties like "Belle of Woking", "Countess of Lovelace", "Veronica's Choice" and "Vyvyan Pennell" together with a rhododendron.

"Huldine" has elegant, pearl white flowers which have a delicate lilac sheen on their undersides. This vigorously growing variety can climb up to 5 m (17 ft).

Garden design

"Perle d'Azur" covers green bushes with its delicate flowers.

"Madame Julia Correvon" (left) and "Victoria" (behind the shrubs).

Clematis and roses

A particularly attractive arrangement is achieved by combining clematis with bush and climbing roses. Both genera have the same requirements in respect to care: both need plenty of water and nutrients.

If you want to grow plants with the same flowering time together, you must take special care that the colours of their flowers will not clash. Flowers in contrasting colours, such as the blue-flowering *Clematis* "The President" with the yellow-flowering climbing rose "Golden Showers", positively glow. A more reserved elegance is achieved with an arrangement in several shades of the same colour; for example, a red-flowering variety like "Niobe" or "Ernest Markham" with the delicate pink flowers of the climbing rose "New Dawn". Other beautiful combinations include:

● the profusely flowering, very healthy climbing rose "New Dawn" with clematis varieties "H. F. Young", "Elsa Späth", "The President" or "Warszawska Nike"

● *Clematis* "Durandii" with pink-flowering wild rose *Rosa rubrifolia*

● *Clematis* "Victoria" with the pink climbing rose "American Pillar"

- *Clematis* "Gipsy Queen" or *Clematis* "H. F. Young" with the velvet red climbing rose "Sympathie"
- *Clematis viticella* "Venosa Violacea" in a white climbing rose
- low-growing *Clematis* "Königskind" at the foot of a white-flowering climbing rose.

My tip: If you decide to grow clematis and roses together you nearly always gain a further advantage in that these combinations appear to flower longer as the flowering times of both plants rarely totally coincide.

Combining climbing plants

Enchanting effects can also be achieved if you plant clematis together with other climbers. The following combine very well:
- *Clematis viticella* "Polish Spirit" or *Clematis viticella* "Etoile Violette" with honeysuckle (*Lonicera x heckrotti* "Goldflame")
- white-flowering *Clematis* "Marie Boisselot" with wild honeysuckle (*Lonicera periclymenum*).

Many beautiful combinations can also be made with different varieties of clematis. For example, try combining the large-flowering, dark *Clematis* "Gipsy Queen" with the small-flowering white *Clematis flammula* or the red *Clematis*

"Ernest Markham" with the dainty *Clematis viticella* "Minuet". Naturally, different large-flowering varieties, like blue *Clematis* "H. F. Young" and white *Clematis* "Marie Boisselot", can be planted together. A splendid display is assured by combining yellow *Clematis tangutica* or *Clematis tibetana vernayi* with *Clematis* "Perle d'Azur" or *Clematis viticella* "Blue Bell".

My tip: Only plant together clematis of the same group (A, B, C, see pp. 16/17) to avoid difficulties in pruning.

Clematis and herbaceous perennials

Some herbaceous perennials produce lovely silvery white leaves, for example dusty miller (*Artemisia stelleriana*), *Stachys byzantina*, sage (*Salvia argentea* or *Salvia juriscii*) and cotton lavender (*Santolina chamaecyparissus*). These almost inconspicuous plants become quite eye-catching if you allow a clematis such as *Clematis viticella* "Etoile Violette" to climb all over them.

Clematis as ground cover

A few clematis varieties (for example *Clematis x jouiniana* and the slightly earlier flowering *Clematis x jouiniana* "Praecox") do not climb, they creep. *Clematis alpina*, *Clematis macropetala* or *Clematis montana* and their varieties can also be used as ground cover.

My tip: A beautiful picture is obtained when a clematis is allowed to spread all over a few very large stones or a single rock and to cover them with a carpet of flowers. Slow-growing species like *Clematis alpina* or *Clematis macropetala* and its varieties are particularly good.

Artificial climbing aids

Whether you wish to utilize existing climbing possibilities or install new climbing aids, using clematis to provide greenery will rapidly make it the visual highlight of your garden.

Fences

A plain wooden or wire fence can be turned into a feature of great beauty when covered in clematis flowers.

Garden design

Depending on the size of the fence, you can plant the luxuriantly growing *Clematis montana*, *Clematis tangutica*, *Clematis tibetana vernayi*, *Clematis viticella* and their varieties or one of the slow-growing garden varieties.

My tip: Choose a clematis from pruning group C (summer-flowering) for a wooden fence that needs regular painting, as this group has to be pruned back radically in the autumn.

Pergolas and free-standing climbing frames

Pergolas, arches and other climbing frames are ideal for clematis to climb on. You can create enchanting scenes if you combine clematis with other climbers. Often, the clematis will find enough to hold on to by climbing up an accompanying plant so that additional tying up or climbing wires will not be needed. Wherever there are no accompanying bushes to provide some hold, additional climbing aids will have to be installed. A wide-mesh wire fence is particularly suitable for this.

Wall espaliers

A wall covered in clematis foliage or a doorway with a clematis arching over makes an attractive eye-catching feature and creates a charming link from garden to house. In this case, climbing aids will almost always be needed and the plants will have to be trained on to them. The right climbing aids for clematis are grids or net-like structures made of wood, wire or strings.

Note
● A wooden espalier should be equipped with additional wire mesh so that the delicate clematis shoots can gain a hold.
● The width of the mesh should not be more than 10 cm (4 in).
● There should be a gap of at least 10 cm (4 in) between the espalier and the wall so that the plants do not suffer from the effects of trapped heat and stale air. If you do not like the idea of having a wall covered in dead leaves and shoots in the autumn, you should choose summer-flowering clematis or clematis of the *viticella* group. They can all be radically cut back in the autumn. Should you wish not to be without some wall covering during the colder months, we recommend combining the clematis with other, evergreen climbing plants like honeysuckle (*Lonicera henryi*). You can also plant a free-standing shrub in front of the wall and allow the clematis to grow into it.

Designing for beginners

Naturally, your choice of clematis will depend entirely on the position available and your own personal preference. However, as an amateur you will avoid disappointments if, beside large-flowering garden varieties, you include in your planting programme more robust types like *Clematis alpina*, *Clematis macropetala*, *Clematis montana*, *Clematis viticella*, *Clematis tangutica* and *Clematis tibetana vernayi* and their varieties. Large-flowering clematis should, if possible, be combined with bush or climbing roses, shrubs or small trees. This will soften the blow if your large-flowering clematis is attacked by clematis wilt (see p. 22).

Clematis montana and its varieties flower profusely in late spring.

A small selection for beginners

We recommend that newcomers to clematis choose a selection that promises a lot of pleasure and little chance of disappointment:

● one variety of *Clematis alpina* or *Clematis macropetala* growing in a bush

● one of the many *Clematis montana* varieties for walls, fences or high trees

● the species *Clematis viticella* or one of its varieties in a large bush or tree. These grow vigorously and flower profusely

● *Clematis tangutica* or *Clematis tibetana vernayi* climbing in a pine tree

● *Clematis versicolor* climbing all over a small bush

● the large-flowering garden varieties "H. F. Young" (mid-blue), "Perle d'Azur" (light blue), "Huldine" (white), "Rouge Cardinal" (red), "Hagley Hybrid" (pink) and "Nelly Moser" (pink). The two last named should not be planted in a position that is too sunny. They are suitable for arches and espaliers but also for climbing up smaller trees or across bushes.

Garden design

"Lady
Northcliffe" with
white-flowering
Hosta
sieboldiana
"Frances
Williams".

Clematis on balconies and patios

Clematis may also decorate balconies and patios if it is planted in large containers. You should, however, choose varieties with a compact growth for growing in this way.

Containers and climbing aids

Containers: Choose glazed clay pots or large containers made of frost-proof terracotta, stone or wood with a diameter of at least 30 cm (12 in) and a height of 40 cm (16 in). It is important to have several drainage holes as clematis are particularly sensitive to waterlogging (see p. 13).

Climbing aids: Various climbing aids for large containers can be found in the specialist trade but they are also easy to make yourself.

Method
● Drive three or four evenly spaced 1 m (40 in) long bamboo sticks into the compost around the outer edge of the pot.
● Link them together at the top with wire and again halfway down.
● Train the clematis shoots upward in many loops around the sticks.
● Contain the growth through targeted cutting back (see pp. 16/17).
● During the winter, clematis in large containers are best kept in a frost-free, bright room.

Clematis for large containers

Generally speaking, any clematis can be planted in a large container. However, very fast-growing specimens will not be kept in check for very long.

The spring-flowering *Clematis alpina* or *Clematis macropetala* and their varieties are suitable for containers but will only flower for a realtively short time.

The early-summer-flowering clematis, whose flowers appear on the previous year's shoots, have particularly compact growth. They are, therefore, best suited for growing in large containers. The following varieties are especially recommended for this method: "Asao", "Dr Ruppel", "Edith", "Elsa Späth", "Haku Ookan", "H. F. Young", "Königskind", "Lasurstern", "Marie Boisselot", "Nelly Moser", "Niobe" and "Vyvyan Pennell".

The summer-flowering clematis form flowers at the ends of the new shoots. They do not, therefore, look quite as dense as the early-summer-flowering ones. The garden varieties "Comtesse de Bouchaud", "General Sikorski", "Hagley Hybrid" and clematis of the *viticella* group are suitable for large containers.

Clematis for vases

Very few florists offer clematis as cut flowers and this means that a clematis used as decoration in a room or as a table ornament on a special occasion will look most original.

Design suggestions
● Stand a single long shoot in an elevated position so that it can hang down as it would naturally.
● The large-flowered varieties look particularly good as a decoration in a vase.
● Create an elegant arrangement combined with branches, roses or hydrangea.
● The fluffy seedheads also make an interesting decoration.

Method
● Choose strong shoots with flowers that are just on the point of opening and remove all superfluous leaves.
● Dip the ends of the stalks in boiling water for about five seconds.
● Before placing them in a vase, stand the stalks as deep as possible in cold water overnight. They will then last for up to eight days. The flowers will not last so long if the stalks are inserted into an oasis or some similar flower arranging aid.

My tip: Even a single clematis shoot without flowers can enhance a bouquet of flowers.

Clematis descriptions

Clematis can be grown in any kind of garden in either a natural or formal setting. The next few pages contain a selection of recommended beauties, grouped according to their flowering times and, therefore, also according to their pruning requirements.

Left: "H. F. Young" presents beautifully formed, delicate blue flowers in early summer.
Above: "Lasurstern" frames a garden seat with its imposing, lavender blue flowers.

Spring-flowering species and varieties

Just when the first delicate flowers of spring arrive to delight us, we are also enchanted by the first flowers of Clematis alpina and Clematis macropetala which open in the second month of spring. Afterwards, in late spring, we admire the profusely flowering, fast-growing varieties of Clematis montana.

Clematis macropetala "Rosy O'Grady".

Clematis alpina

This indigenous European species grows in the Alps up to elevations of about 2,500 m (over 8,300 ft).

Flower: Violet blue, bell-like, pendulous. The petals of the wild form are 3-4 cm (1¼-1½ in) long, and up to 6 cm (2¼ in) long in the varieties. Pretty seedheads.
Flowering time: Middle to late spring. At higher altitudes, early to mid-summer.
Height of growth: Up to 2.5 m (8 ft).
Country of origin: European Alps, Norway to Siberia.
Position: Suitable for all positions, will also cope with shade.

Growth: Will climb on small trees, shrubs and walls.
Garden varieties: Often offered for sale:
● "Columbine", pale blue
● "Frances Rivis", pale blue
● "Pamela Jackman", dark blue
● "Ruby", dark purple pink
Rarely offered:
● "Jacqueline du Pré", red with white edges
● "White Columbine", white
● "Willy", pale pink

Clematis macropetala

This species, originating from the Far East, is a tireless climber and completely hardy.

Flower: Blue violet with four petals, bell-like, pendulous. Numerous staminodes (petal-like stamens) appear on the inside, similar in colour to the petals, making the flowers look almost double. Decorative seedheads.
Flowering time: Late spring to early summer.
Height of growth: Up to 3 m (10 ft).

"Pamela Jackman".

"Ruby".

Country of origin:
Northern China, Siberia
and Mongolia.
Position: Suitable for
any position.
Garden varieties:
● "Floralia", blue
● "Georg", blue
● "Helsingborg",
purple
● "Jan Lindmark", pink
purple
● "Maidwell Hall", dark
blue
● "Markham's Pink",
pink
● "Rodklokke",
pinkish-red
● "Rosy O'Grady",
brilliant pink
● "Snowbird", white
● "Veronica", blue
● "White Swan", pure
white
● "White Tokyo", white

Clematis macropetala "Maidwell Hall" is robust and easy to grow.

Clematis montana

Flower: The wild form
of this species has a
white flower with narrow
petals and yellow
stamens; the varieties
are white or pink with
up to 6 cm (2¼ in) large
flowers and usually four
petals. Some varieties
are scented.
Flowering time:
Depending on the
variety of this species,
between late spring and
early summer, for about
14 days.
Height of growth: Up
to 10 m (33 ft).

Country of origin:
Middle and western
China, Himalayas.
Position: Suitable for
any position.
Growth: This fast-
growing climber is just
right for covering up
old sheds, old fruit trees
that no longer bear fruit,
fences or house walls
with a grand profusion
of leaves and flowers.
My tip: Young plants
may be at risk from late
frosts in some areas.
Garden varieties:
● "Freda", pink
flowers, bronze-
coloured leaves

● "Grandiflora", white,
scented
● "Picton's Variety",
pink; only up to 6 m
(20 ft) tall
● "Pink Perfection",
pink flowers with a
strong scent
● "Tetrarose" (see
inside front cover/p. 1),
pink
● "Rubens", pink
● *Clematis montana*
var. *wilsonii*, white,
scented flowers in early
summer

"Rubens".

Large-flowered, early-summer-flowering clematis

When talking about clematis, one usually thinks of a mass of large, white, red or violet blue flowers on an arch or pergola. These large-flowered varieties first became stars among the climbing plants as early as the nineteenth century, which is why there are hundreds of them today.

"Marie Boisselot" has glowing white flowers.

These varieties are derived from crosses between *Clematis lanuginosa*, *Clematis patens* and *Clematis florida* and belong to group B (see pp. 16/17). Usually, they are not great climbers and 3 m (10 ft) is about their limit. This means that they are very suitable for cultivating in large containers. The large flowers, which are double in some varieties, require a lot of attention when planting and regular care thereafter. A position sheltered from the wind or a shrub as a support for the flowers would be ideal. In ideal conditions and favourable weather you may expect a second flowering during early autumn.

"Marie Boisselot"

Often offered under the name "Mme Le Coultre".
Flower: Pure white with yellow stamens, has delicate greenish stripes when the flower opens out. Diameter of flower up to 18 cm (7 in).
Flowering time: Early summer with a second flowering in early autumn.
Height of growth: 3 m (10 ft).
Position: Suitable for any position.
My tip: This particularly beautiful, white variety will also look very good in a shady position.

"Miss Bateman"

Flower: Creamy white with dark purple stamens. Diameter of flower about 12 cm (4¾ in).
Flowering time: Early summer with a second flowering in early autumn.
Height of growth: 2 m (7 ft).
Position: Suitable for any position.

"Snow Queen"

Flower: Snow white with a bluish tinge and dark brown stamens. Diameter of flower up to 15 cm (6 in).

"Miss Bateman".

Flowering time: Late spring/early summer with a second flowering in early autumn.
Height of growth: 2.5-3 m (8-10 ft).
Position: Not suitable for purely north-facing positions.
Growth: Particularly suitable for large containers.

"Edith"

Flower: White with dark brown stamens. Slightly yellowish central stripe that turns pale later on. Diameter 10-12 cm (4-4¾ in).
Flowering time: Early summer with a second flowering in early autumn.
Height of growth: 2 m (7 ft).
Position: This variety is not suitable for purely

"Snow Queen" produces attractive white flowers with dark stamens.

north-facing positions.
Growth: Ideal for large containers as it has very compact growth.
My tip: Forms attractive seedheads.

"Duchess of Edinburgh"

Flower: Double white flowers with yellow stamens. Diameter to 12 cm (4¾ in).
Flowering time: Late spring/early summer with a second flowering in early autumn.
Height of growth: 2.5-3.5 m (8-12 ft).
Position: Suitable for any position.
My tip: The long-lasting flowers are particularly suitable for displaying in vases.

Other varieties

● "Alabast", with white, double flowers and dark blue stamens
● "Belle of Woking", flower white, slight lilac tinge, single or double
● "Fair Rosamund", white flowers with slight pink tinge, faintly scented
● "Henryi", creamy white flowers with reddish-brown stamens
● "Moonlight", pale yellow flowers. Not for south-facing positions

"Edith".

"Duchess of Edinburgh".

Clematis descriptions

"Warszawska Nike"

Flower: Deep purple with yellow stamens. Diameter up to 15 cm (6 in). Profusely flowering.
Flowering time: Early summer, single flowers until early autumn.
Height of growth: 3 m (10 ft).
Position: Not for north-facing positions.
Growth: The dark flowers require a light background.

"Dr Ruppel"

Flower: Deep pink with central stripe and cream-coloured stamens. Thick petals, slightly wavy, diameter of flower up to 18 cm (7 in).
Flowering time: Early summer, later flowers in early autumn.
Height of growth: 3 m (10 ft).
Position: Vigorously growing, not suitable for purely south-facing positions.
My tip: A profusely flowering variety.

"Warszawska Nike".

"Bees' Jubilee"

Flower: Mallow pink with a carmine red central stripe and brown stamens. Diameter up to 16 cm (6½ in).
Flowering time: Early summer, second flowering in early autumn.
Height of growth: 2.5 m (8 ft).
Position: Prefers semi-shade; not for south-facing positions.
My tip: Will only grow slowly to begin with.

"Nelly Moser"

Flower: Mallow pink with a violet central stripe and red stamens. Diameter up to 18 cm (7 in).

"Dr Ruppel".

Flowering time: Early summer with a second flowering in early autumn.
Height of growth: 3 m (10 ft).
Position: Semi-shady.
Growth: Looks best in front of a quiet background.

"Niobe"

Flower: Dark red with yellow stamens. Diameter of flower about 15 cm (6 in).
Flowering time: Early summer with a second flowering in early autumn.
Height of growth: 2.5 m (8 ft).
Growth: Suitable for large containers. Requires regular light pruning.
My tip: An unusually beautiful variety which flowers profusely and for a long time.

"Bees' Jubilee".

Large-flowered, early-summer-flowering varieties in red and pink

"Niobe".

Other varieties

- "Asao", dark pink, profusely flowering
- "Barbara Dibley", strong petunia red with dark central stripe
- "Carnaby", petunia red, white edges
- "Charissima", cherry red with a dark central stripe; profusely flowering
- "Jackmanii Rubra", semi-double, petunia red flowers; profusely flowering, flowers for a long time
- "King Edward VII", violet red
- "Maureen", red violet flowers with a red central stripe; flowers for a long time

"Nelly Moser" has striking, violet central stripes.

Clematis descriptions

"Lasurstern"

Flower: Lavender blue with cream-coloured stamens. Beautiful flowers with 7-8 petals, wavy edges. Diameter up to 18 cm (7 in).
Flowering time: Late spring/early summer with a second flowering in early autumn.
Height of growth: 2.5 m (8 ft).
Position: Not for purely north-facing positions.
My tip: With the right care, a mature plant may bear up to 100 flowers.

"Haku Ookan"

Flower: Deep blue violet with white stamens, 8 quite narrow petals which makes the flower look single to semi-double. Diameter 15 cm (6 in).
Flowering time: Early summer; a second flowering in early autumn.
Height of growth: 2.5 m (8 ft).
Position: Not suitable for purely north-facing positions.
My tip: Particularly attractive as cut flowers.

"Lasurstern" is a tried and tested early-flowering variety.

"Mrs N. Thompson"

Flower: Blue purple with a red central stripe and red stamens. Diameter up to 15 cm (6 in).
Flowering time: Early summer; a second flowering in early autumn.
Height of growth: 2.5-3.5 m (8-12 ft).
Position: Not for north-facing positions.
Growth: A solitary position is recommended.
My tip: Slightly sensitive variety; grows slowly to begin with.

"Elsa Späth".

Large-flowered, early-summer-flowering varieties in blue, violet and purple

"Haku Ookan" will thrive in a large container.

"Mrs N. Thompson" is slightly sensitive.

"Elsa Späth"

Flower: Blue violet with wide, overlapping petals and red stamens. Diameter up to 18 cm (7 in).
Flowering time: Early summer; second flowering in early autumn.
Height of growth: 2.5 m (8 ft).
Position: Suitable for all positions.
My tip: Flowers profusely and for a long time. Problem-free, so good for beginners.

"Mrs Cholmondeley"

Flower: Lavender blue with brown stamens. Long, narrow petals. Diameter up to 18 cm (7 in).
Flowering time: Early summer; carries on flowering until early autumn.

"Mrs Cholmondeley".

Height of growth: 4 m (13 ft).
Position: Suitable for any position.
Growth: Versatile and suitable for arches and pergolas together with red and white flowering roses.
My tip: Flowers profusely. Ideal for beginners.

Other varieties

● "Alice Fisk", wisteria-blue flowers with long, pointed petals with wavy edges and brown stamens
● "Beauty of Worcester", dark blue with a light-coloured back and yellow stamens, double, profusely flowering
● "Countess of Lovelace", double, rosette-shaped flowers, lavender blue with white stamens; requires time
● "Daniel Deronda", purple blue, semi-double flowers with a light central stripe; single second flowers
● "H. F. Young" (see pp. 34/35), mid-blue with cream-coloured stamens, profusely flowering
● "Kathleen Wheeler", 8 plum-blue petals with light-coloured stamens; the flowers are sensitive to wind

Clematis descriptions

"Vyvyan Pennell"

Flower: Lavender blue, very double, with yellow stamens. Diameter about 15 cm (6 in). The second flowers are single!
Flowering time: Early summer with a second flowering in late summer/early autumn.
Height of growth: 3 m (10 ft).
Position: Not for purely north-facing positions.
Growth: Sheltered from wind and best planted in such a way that the double flowers are supported by a shrub (e.g. rhododendron, star magnolia).

"The President"

Flower: Purple blue with reddish-brown stamens. 8 petals, flower diameter up to 18 cm (7 in).
Flowering time: Early summer with a second flowering in early autumn.
Height of growth: 3 m (10 ft).
Position: Suitable for all positions.
My tip: Flowers profusely and for a long time. A standard variety is frequently offered for sale.

The lively, double flowers of "Vyvyan Pennell".

"The President".

"Königskind".

"Königskind"

Flower: Light or dark blue violet with white filaments and violet black anthers. Diameter about 10 cm (4 in).
Flowering time: Early summer to mid-autumn with interruptions.
Height of growth: Up to 2 m (7 ft).
Position: Suitable for any position.
Growth: Particularly suitable for growing over low bushes and for cultivating in large containers.
My tip: The colour of the flower may vary, depending on the soil consistency, between royal blue to lavender blue.

"Lady Northcliffe"

Flower: Blue with yellow stamens. Diameter up to 15 cm (6 in).
Flowering time: Early summer; a second flowering in early autumn.
Height of growth: About 2 m (7 ft).
Position: Not for north-facing positions.
My tip: Flowers profusely.

Large-flowered, early-summer-flowering varieties in blue, violet and purple

"Lady Northcliffe" flowers profusely and tirelessly.

Other varieties

● "Lady Caroline Nevill", lavender blue, semi-double flowers
● "Miriam Markham", lavender blue, double flowers, not many but very beautiful; flowers for a long time
● "Mrs James Mason", violet blue, double flowers with a red central stripe and light-coloured filaments
● "Prins Hendrik", 7 short, wide, wavy petals in lavender blue with a dark central stripe and dark stamens
● "Richard Pennell", 8 wavy petals, purple blue, profusely flowering, robust and beautiful!
● "Walter Pennell" (see p. 25), blue pink with a dark central stripe and light-coloured stamens; expressive semi-double flowers
● "Wilhelmina Tull", violet with reddish central stripe

"Multi Blue"

Flower: Densely double, dark blue flowers with lighter, twirled tips. Diameter about 15 cm (6 in).
Flowering time: Early summer; carries on flowering through to early autumn.

"Multi Blue".

Height of growth: 3 m (10 ft).
Position: Suitable for any position.
My tip: An unusual and attractive new cultivar!

Large-flowered, summer-flowering clematis

The classic representative of this group is Clematis "Jackmanii", a cultivar that was created over 100 years ago and is still to be found in many gardens. The clematis varieties of this group flower later and usually grow more vigorously than the early-summer-flowering ones. They are excellent for climbing through trees.

Most clematis varieties of this group are derived from *Clematis* "Jackmanii". In all of them, the flowers are formed on the new shoots of the current year's wood, so they belong in group C (see pp. 16/17).

Some varieties of this group do not flower until very late, even as late as early and mid-autumn, for example "Lady Betty Balfour". They require a warm, bright position in order to form their flowers before the cool nights of early autumn.

The velvety red flowers of "Rouge Cardinal".

"Rouge Cardinal"

Flower: Crimson with reddish-brown stamens. Flower diameter about 10 cm (4 in).
Flowering time: Mid-summer to early autumn.
Height of growth: 3 m (10 ft).
Position: Not for purely north-facing positions.
My tip: A profusely flowering, robust variety with compact growth and a long flowering time.

"Allanah"

Flower: Flowing dark red flowers with brown stamens. 8 petals, diameter about 12 cm (4¾ in).
Flowering time: Early summer, then flowering less profusely into early autumn.
Height of growth: 4 m (13 ft).
Position: Not suitable for north-facing positions.
My tip: A robust, younger variety that has still to be tested fully.

"Huldine"

Flower: Faintly lilac-tinged white. Flower diameter about 8 cm (3¼ in).
Flowering time: Late summer to early autumn.

Height of growth: 5 m (17 ft).
Position: Particularly vigorously growing, suitable for sunny positions. Not for purely north-facing positions.

"Allanah".

"Hagley Hybrid"

Flower: Mallow pink with reddish-brown stamens. Flower diameter 8-13 cm (3¼-5 in).
Flowering time: Mid to late summer.
Height of growth: 2.5 m (8 ft).
Position: Not suitable for purely south-facing positions.
Growth: The delicate pink looks good with dark or grey blue conifers.
My tip: A variety that flowers profusely and for a long time, with a compact shape of growth. Very suitable for beginners. The mallow pink flowers start out a deep shade that later becomes paler.

"Huldine" prefers a sunny position.

"Ville de Lyon"

Flower: Carmine red with yellow stamens. Flower diameter about 12 cm (4¾ in).
Flowering time: Mid-summer to early autumn.
Height of growth: 4 m (13 ft).
Position: Not suitable for purely north-facing positions.
My tip: This variety requires plenty of water and fertilizer for profuse flowering.

Other varieties

● "John Paul II", flower pale pinkish-white
● "John Huxtable", white; the oldest white variety among the summer-flowering clematis hybrids
● "Comtesse de Bouchaud" (see pp. 24/25), mallow pink, problem-free, profusely flowering variety
● "Ernest Markham", 6 broad, dark red petals
● "Madame Edouard André", red, beautifully formed flowers
● "Madame Julia Correvon" (see p. 10), wine red flowers
● "Star of India", purple with central red stripe

"Hagley Hybrid".

"Ville de Lyon".

Clematis descriptions

"Perle d'Azur"

Flower: Light blue with creamy white to greenish stamens. Flower diameter about 10 cm (4 in).
Flowering time: Mid-summer to early autumn.
Height of growth: 4.5 m (15 ft).
Position: Suitable for any position.
Growth: Particularly beautiful if it is allowed to grow into a red-leafed ornamental cherry tree.
My tip: A top class variety.

"Jackmanii"

Flower: Blue purple with greenish stamens. Diameter about 10 cm (4 in).
Flowering time: Mid to late summer.
Height of growth: 3 m (10 ft).
Position: Suitable for any position.
Growth: Effective with red and yellow roses.
My tip: "Jackmanii" is the classic among cultivars. This variety, created by Jackman in Britain in 1863, started the success story of the large-flowered garden varieties (see pp. 4/5). The similar variety "Jackmanii Superba" has slightly larger, darker and wider petals.

"Perle d'Azur" has slightly rolled back petals.

"Durandii"

Flower: Indigo blue, diameter up to 12 cm (4¾ in).
Flowering time: Mid to late summer.
Height of growth: About 2 m (7 ft). Does not climb!
Position: Suitable for any position.

"Jackmanii".

Growth: As it will not climb, you can either allow it to creep over low-growing shrubs or tie it to a free-standing pillar.

My tip: Will flower particularly profusely if given plenty of fertilizer. An attractive cut flower. It can be propagated through division like a herbaceous perennial clematis (see p. 20).

"Gipsy Queen"

Flower: Dark purple with red stamens. Beautiful flower shape, diameter about 12 cm (4¾ in).

Flowering time: Late summer to early autumn.

Height of growth: 3.5 m (12 ft).

Position: Not suitable for purely north-facing positions.

"Durandii" is a consistently flowering variety that does not climb.

Growth: Grown together with *Clematis flammula* (see p. 54) in a sunny position, it creates a very effective picture.

"Lady Betty Balfour"

Flower: Purple blue with yellow stamens. Flower diameter about 15 cm (6 in).

Flowering time: Early to middle autumn.

Height of growth: 4.5 m (15 ft).

Position: You can only be certain of obtaining flowers in a warm, sunny position.

My tip: This particularly late-flowering variety may well become a highlight in your autumn garden.

Other varieties

● "Ascotiensis", glowing blue flowers with light-coloured stamens
● "Prince Charles", pinkish-blue, profusely flowering
● "Rhapsody", new variety. Star-shaped, intensely blue flowers from mid-summer to early autumn

"Gipsy Queen".

"Lady Betty Balfour".

Clematis viticella and its varieties

In addition to the large-flowered garden varieties, there are also many attractive, small-flowering clematis that were created from the wild species Clematis viticella. They are strong and robust, almost completely resistant to clematis wilt and suitable for formal and nature gardens.

Clematis viticella, the Italian wild clematis, originates from southern Europe and Asia Minor. Its graceful, pendulous flowers are up to 6 cm (2¼ in) across and flower in shades of lilac to mauve. The flowers appear in their hundreds from mid-summer to early autumn and nod in the wind on long stalks. This clematis is eminently suitable for growing through shrubs or trees. The wild species, as well as all garden varieties derived from it, belongs to group C (see pp. 16/17). Unfortunately, they are only rarely available in the trade but they can usually be obtained from specialist mail-order firms (see addresses, p. 61).

"Purpurea Plena Elegans"

Flower: Soft red, double. Diameter 5 cm (2 in).
Flowering time: Mid-summer to early autumn.
Height of growth: 3.5 m (12 ft).
Position: Not for north-facing positions.
Growth: Flowers should be seen from close up.

"Etoile Violette"

Flower: Dark violet with yellow stamens; diameter up to 10 cm (4 in). Very profusely flowering.
Flowering time: Mid-summer to early autumn.
Height of growth: 4 m (13 ft).
Position: Any.

"Purpurea Plena Elegans".

"Abundance"

Flower: Deep pink, diameter up to 5 cm (2 in).
Flowering time: Mid-summer to early autumn.
Height of growth: Up to 4 m (13 ft).
Position: Not for north-facing positions.

"Abundance".

Small-flowered, summer-flowering *Clematis viticella* and its varieties

"Alba Luxurians"

Flower: White with dark stamens, often with green specks. Diameter to 9 cm (3½ in).
Flowering time: Mid-summer to early autumn.
Height of growth: Up to 3 m (10 ft).
Position: Not for north-facing positions.
Growth: Attractive with dark-foliaged companion plants; for example, holly.

"Rubra"

Flower: Warm red with reddish-brown stamens. Diameter 5 cm (2 in).
Flowering time: Mid-summer to early autumn.
Height of growth: 3.5 m (12 ft).
Position: Not for north-facing positions.
Growth: Will climb well in shrubs that are not too tall; for example, dogwood (*Cornus*).

Other varieties

● "Betty Corning", pale blue, bell-shaped flowers; flowers for a long time
● "Little Nell", white with pale pink edges

The enchanting "Etoile Violette" flowers profusely.

"Alba Luxurians".

"Rubra".

● "Minuet", white flowers with pink edges
● "Polish Spirit", new variety with deep violet flowers; vigorously growing
● "Royal Velours", purple red
● "Venosa Violacea", white with purple violet edges and veins

Herbaceous perennials and *Clematis texensis*

In addition to the many climbing clematis, a number of herbaceous perennials also belong to the large genus of Clematis. As they themselves do not climb, they require a climbing aid or support. The group Clematis texensis and its varieties is particularly unusual in its flower shapes and colours.

Clematis integrifolia "Blue Bell".

Clematis integrifolia

Flower: Blue, pendulous bells with long, pointed petals. About 3 cm (1¼ in) long.
Flowering time: Early to late summer.
Height of growth: About 1 m (40 in).
Country of origin: South-west Russia, western and central Asia.
Position: Requires a sunny position.
Growth: Produces lots of shoots and needs to be supported, for example with a wire at the foot of an arch.
Garden varieties:
● "Alba", white
● "Blue Bell", blue
● "Rosea", pink
● "Olgae", pale blue

Clematis heracleifolia

The leaves and entire shoot system of this species are so vigorous and strong that they would not suit a very elegant, formal garden.
Flower: Graceful, small, blue bells, up to 2.5 cm (1 in).
Flowering time: Mid-summer to early autumn.
Height of growth: About 1 m (40 in) tall.
Country of origin: Northern and central China.
Position: Not for north-facing positions.
Garden varieties:
● "Campanile", blue.
● "Davidiana", light blue, scented.
● "Wyevale", blue, scented.

Clematis x jouiniana

Flower: Small, lilac-coloured stars, up to 2.5 cm (1 in).
Flowering time: Late summer to mid-autumn.
Height of growth: About 2 m (7 ft).
Position: Not for north-facing positions.

Clematis texensis.

Clematis heracleifolia "Wyevale".

Clematis jouiniana "Praecox".

Growth: Good as ground cover or for covering a low fence.
My tip: I recommend the variety "Praecox" which flowers earlier than the species.

Clematis texensis

This still relatively unknown and unusual species deserves much more attention.
Flower: Up to 2.5 cm (1 in) long, tulip-shaped small bells in deep red with light-coloured petal tips. The flowers of varieties are larger but all possess the characteristic tulip shape.
Flowering time: Mid-

summer to mid-autumn.
Height of growth:
2-3 m (7-10 ft).
Country of origin:
Texas, USA.
Position: Both the wild species, as well as the garden varieties derived from it, require a warm, sunny, airy position.
Growth: Good for covering low-growing

"The Princess of Wales".

shrubs with flowers.
My tip: A light covering of dead leaves is recommended as winter protection.
Other varieties:
● "Duchess of Albany", pink flower with red stripes and light-coloured stamens, diameter up to 5 cm (2 in)
● "Etoile Rose", red flowers with a light-coloured edge; diameter up to 5 cm (2 in). Particularly vigorously growing and profusely flowering
● "Gravetye Beauty", beautiful, deep red flowers up to 6 cm (2¼ in)
● "Sir Trevor Lawrence", the flowers

are deep red on the inside, light on the outside
● "The Princess of Wales", brilliant red, particularly beautiful new variety

Other species

The following species also have bell-shaped or urn-shaped flowers:
● *Clematis versicolor*, mallow pink
● *Clematis pitcheri*, purple violet
● *Clematis crispa*, pale blue
● *Clematis viorna*, reddish-purple

Other small-flowered species and varieties

The summer-flowering species introduced here are vigorously growing and unfold their star- or bell-shaped flowers between mid-summer and early autumn. There are many shades of white and yellow in this group, from pale primrose right through to bright orange yellow.

All the species and varieties named here are often propagated from seed. In this case, however, the size of the flower and its colour and scent will no longer correspond exactly to the details given here.

Clematis flammula

Flower: Star-shaped white flowers, about 4 cm (1½ in). Strong scent. Profusely flowering.
Flowering time: Late summer to early autumn.
Height of growth: Up to 6 m (20 ft).
Country of origin: Southern Europe, Asia Minor.
Position: Suitable for any position.
Growth: Suitable for growing through shrubs

Clematis tibetana vernayi

Often displayed in nurseries as *Clematis orientalis* (see pp. 62/63).
Flower: Nodding, yellow flowers with thick petals; diameter about 2 cm (¾ in).
Flowering time: Mid-summer to mid-autumn.
Height of growth: About 5 m (17 ft).
Country of origin: Northern India.
Position: Not suitable for purely north-facing positions.
Growth: Very charming when combined with conifers.
Garden varieties:
● "Bill Mackenzie", with glowing yellow flowers, up to 5 cm (2 in). Attractive seedheads

The dainty, starlike flowers of Clematis flammula.

● "Orange Peel" with flowers in a soft, pleasant yellow. The petals are thick and fleshy which is what gives it its variety name (see pp. 3 and 15)

Clematis rehderiana.

Clematis rehderiana

Flower: Small, bell-like, pale yellow flowers. Strong scent.
Flowering time: Mid-summer to mid-autumn.
Height of growth: Up to 6 m (20 ft).
Country of origin: Western China.
Position: Not for purely north-facing positions.

Clematis potaninii var. potaninii

Previously *Clematis fargesii* var. *souliei*.
Flower: White flowers, diameter 4 cm (1½ in).
Flowering time: Mid-summer to early autumn.
Height of growth: 5 m (17 ft).
Country of origin: China.
Position: Any.

The nodding yellow flowers of Clematis tibetana vernayi "Orange Peel".

Clematis potaninii.

"Rubromarginata".

Clematis x triternata "Rubromarginata"

Flower: A mass of 2.5 cm (1 in) white-pink stars. Scented.
Flowering time: Mid-summer to early autumn
Height of growth: 5 m (17 ft).
Position: Any.

Other species

● *Clematis tangutica*, yellow flowers with pointed petals, up to 5 cm (2 in). Will only produce profuse flowers in full sunlight. Particularly attractive is the variety "Aureolin", with deep yellow flowers up to 7 cm (2¾ in).

Novelties and rarities

During the last few years, numerous beautiful clematis varieties have been created in Western Europe, Estonia, Poland, Russia, Sweden and Japan. In addition, there are some particularly attractive exotic varieties which are, unfortunately, not quite hardy in a temperate climate. A selection of most attractive representatives of these groups is introduced here.

An attractive new variety called "Violetta".

"Violetta"
Raiser: Westphal (Germany), 1994.
Flower: Rose violet with dark veins. Diameter about 12 cm (4¾ in).
Flowering time: Mid to late spring and late summer.
Height of growth: 3 m (10 ft).
Position: Any.
Group: B.

"Arctic Queen"
Raiser: R. Evison (England), 1994.
Flower: White, double flowers with yellow stamens. Diameter about 15 cm (6 in).
Flowering time: Early summer; again in late summer/early autumn.
Height of growth: 2 m (7 ft).

Position: Sheltered from the wind.
Group: B.
My tip: A profusely flowering variety, suitable for growing in a large container!

"Aljonushka"

A herbaceous perennial that was raised in the Soviet Union in 1963.
Flower: Deep mallow pink. Diameter 6 cm (2½ in).
Flowering time: Mid-summer to mid-autumn.
Height of growth: Up to 2 m (7 ft).
Position: Sunny, not for purely north-facing positions.
Group: C.

Other new varieties

Large-flowered, summer-flowering varieties (all in group C):
● "Arabella", raiser: Fretwell, Britain. Purple blue with a red central stripe, diameter about 8 cm (3¼ in). Flowers early summer to mid-autumn; height of growth 2 m (7 ft).

"Arctic Queen".

"Aljonushka".

● "Romantika", raiser: Kivistik, Estonia. Dark violet flowers, diameter 13 cm (5 in), flowers from early summer to early autumn, height 2 m (7 ft)

● "Yukikomachi", cultivar from Japan. White, purple tinge along flower edges. Diameter 10 cm (4 in); flowers from late summer to middle autumn, height 3 m (10 ft)

Small-flowered

Two varieties from the *alpina* group (group A) come from the famous Swedish clematis raiser Magnus Johnson. They are also suitable for higher altitudes:

● "Georg", blue violet; flowering time mid-spring to early summer; second flowering until mid-autumn

● "Albinaplena", white; flowering time mid-spring to early summer; second flowering until mid-autumn

Clematis florida "Sieboldii"

Flower: Unusual and exotic flowers, white with purple centres.

Exotic Clematis florida "Sieboldii" will thrive in a large container.

Diameter about 8 cm (3¼ in). In addition, there is the variety "Plena" with white, double flowers.

Flowering time: Early summer to early autumn.

"Apple Blossom".

Height of growth: Up to 3 m (10 ft).

Position: Outside, on a warm, sheltered house wall, best in a large container. For greenhouse and a cool conservatory.

Group: C.

Growth: Choose an attractive pot or pot holder that will underline the beauty of these flowers.

My tip: Overwinter container plants in a cool, frost-free room. They will not mind a dark cellar room.

Clematis armandii

Flower: Scented white flowers. Diameter about 5 cm (2 in).

Flowering time: Early to mid-spring.

Height of growth: Up to 6 m (20 ft).

Country of origin: Central and western China.

Position: This vigorously growing species and its varieties "Apple Blossom" and "Snowdrift" can only be grown in a large greenhouse.

Group: A.

Clematis descriptions

Purple pink flowering "Victoria" belongs among the early-summer-flowering clematis varieties.

Index

Figures given in bold indicate
illustrations.

aphids 22

Index

Further reading and addresses

Further reading

(If not obtainable in book shops, try libraries.)

Evison, R., *Making the most of Clematis*, Floraprint, Wisbech
Fisk, J., *Clematis, The Queen of Climbers*, Cassell, London
Fretwell, B., *Clematis as Companion Plants*, Cassell, London
Lloyd, C., *Clematis*, Penguin Books, London

Acknowledgements

The author and publishers would like to thank Friedrich M. Westphal for his friendly and expert advice.

Author's notes

This volume deals with the care of clematis in the garden, on patios or in a greenhouse. Just like several other members of the Ranunculaceae family, clematis contain the substance protoanemonin. This is a skin irritant and will also cause abdominal cramps if taken internally. For this reason, always wear gloves if you have an open wound and are handling clematis. Do not chew leaves or stalks and do not consume any other parts of the plants. Make absolutely sure that children and domestic pets do not eat any parts of the plant.

If you should injure yourself while handling soil, visit a physician and get expert treatment. Discuss with him or her the possibility of having a tetanus vaccination. When using plant protection agents, follow the instructions on the packaging meticulously. Store plant protection agents and fertilizers (including organic ones) in such a way that they are inaccessible to children and domestic pets. Consumption of such substances can lead to damage to health.

Also make sure that these substances never get into your eyes.

Photographic acknowledgements

The photos in this volume were taken by Marion Nickig, with the exception of:
Cover photography by L. Rose, Photos Horticultural Picture Library.
Evison: p. 56 bottom;
Horsch: p. 53 bottom, 57 top;
Jensen: p. 57 bottom;
Schneiders: p. 31.

Cover photographs

Front cover: *Clematis "Capitaine Thuilleaux", Clematis "Madame Edouard Andre", Clematis "Lasurstern", Clematis "Myojo".*
Inside front cover: *Clematis montana "Tetrarose" (see p. 37);*
Back cover: *Clematis montana "Rubens".*

Reprinted 1998

This edition published by Merehurst Limited,
Ferry House, 51-57 Lacy Road, Putney, London SW15 1PR

Reprinted 1997
© 1992 Gräfe und Unzer GmbH, Munich

A catalogue record for this book is available from the British Library.

English text copyright © Merehurst Limited 1996
Translated by Astrid Mick
Edited by Lesley Young
Design and typesetting by Paul Cooper Design
Printed in Hong Kong by Wing King Tong

Fascinating seedheads

This is a typical example of the fluffy seedheads formed by many clematis but particularly the wild species after they have finished flowering. In some species, like the indigenous European traveller's joy (*Clematis vitalba*), they may even beat the flower for beauty.

The fragile, soft, hairy, elongated seed capsules are carried off by the wind to provide a means of distribution of the seed.

The silky-soft seedheads of Clematis tibetana vernayi "Orange Peel" shimmer in the late summer sunlight.